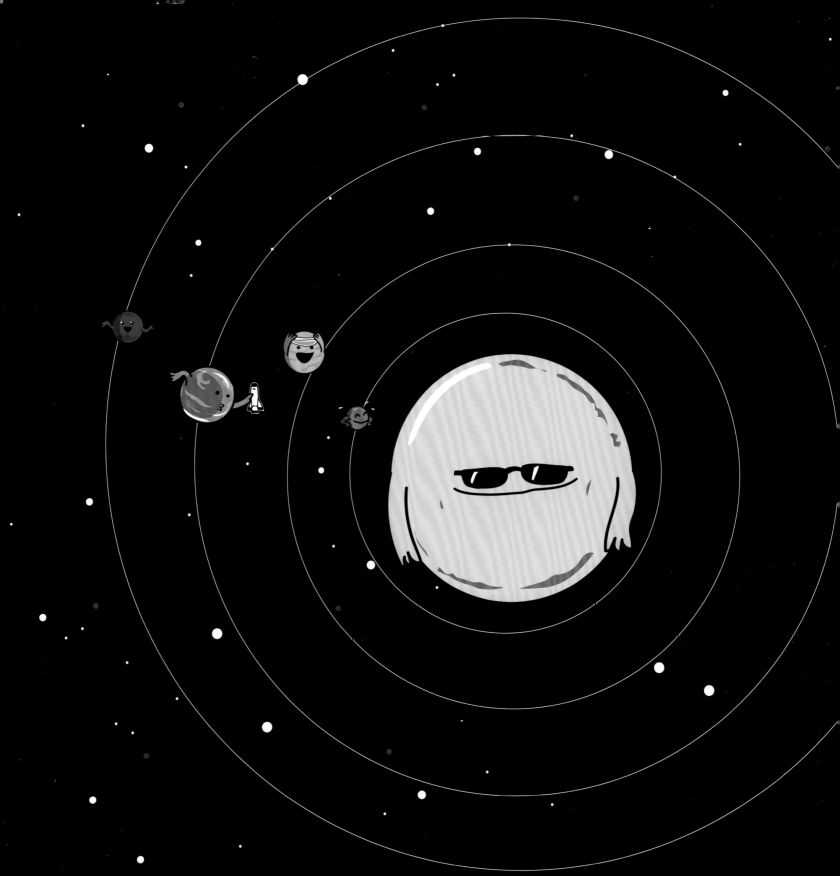

THE SUN IS KIND OF A BIG DEAL

Nick Seluk

Scholastic Children's Books

All of the **planets** and the **Sun** live together in the **solar system** like a big family.

The Sun is our solar system's very own **STAR**!

Seriously! The Sun is an *actual* star! It's the only star in our solar system, and it sits right in the centre, holding everything together.

SO, WHAT'S IN THE SOLAR SYSTEM BESIDES THE SUN AND THE PLANETS?

* **Dwarf planets** – five rocky bodies that are smaller than planets
* **Asteroids** – small, rocky objects that move around between Mars and Jupiter in the "asteroid belt"
* **Meteors** – streaks of light created when pieces of space rock or metal speed into Earth's atmosphere (If you see a shooting star, it's actually a meteor!)
* **Comets** – icy rocks that shoot through space and leave a trail of gas and dust
* **Aliens** – okay, maybe not, but we're always looking for them!

Saturn

Uranus

Neptune

OH HEY, GUESS WHAT?

Our solar system is just one of MANY solar systems that exist. A **galaxy** is a group made up of billions of solar systems. Our galaxy is called the Milky Way. There are BILLIONS of galaxies out there, and together they make up the universe. Can *you* count to a billion?

The Sun is the biggest thing
in the solar system.

It's even bigger than Earth!

Way bigger.
Way, way bigger.
Like, over a million times bigger!

There are much bigger stars than the Sun, but all of the other stars you see are

really

really

really

really far away.

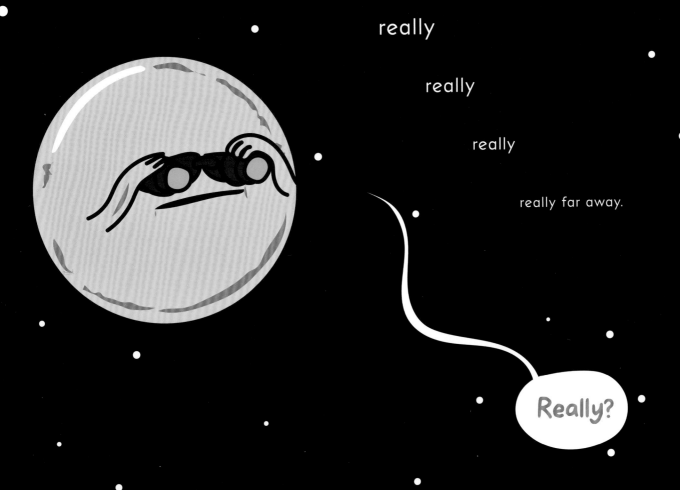

Really. The other stars are in totally different solar systems and have their own planets.

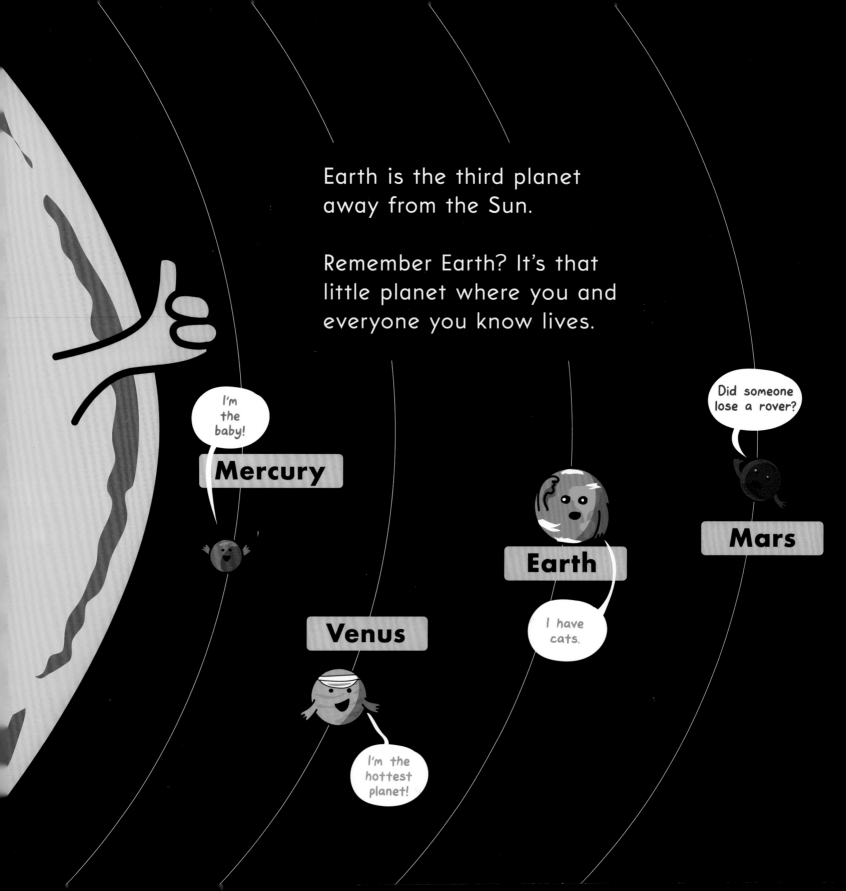

Earth is the third planet away from the Sun.

Remember Earth? It's that little planet where you and everyone you know lives.

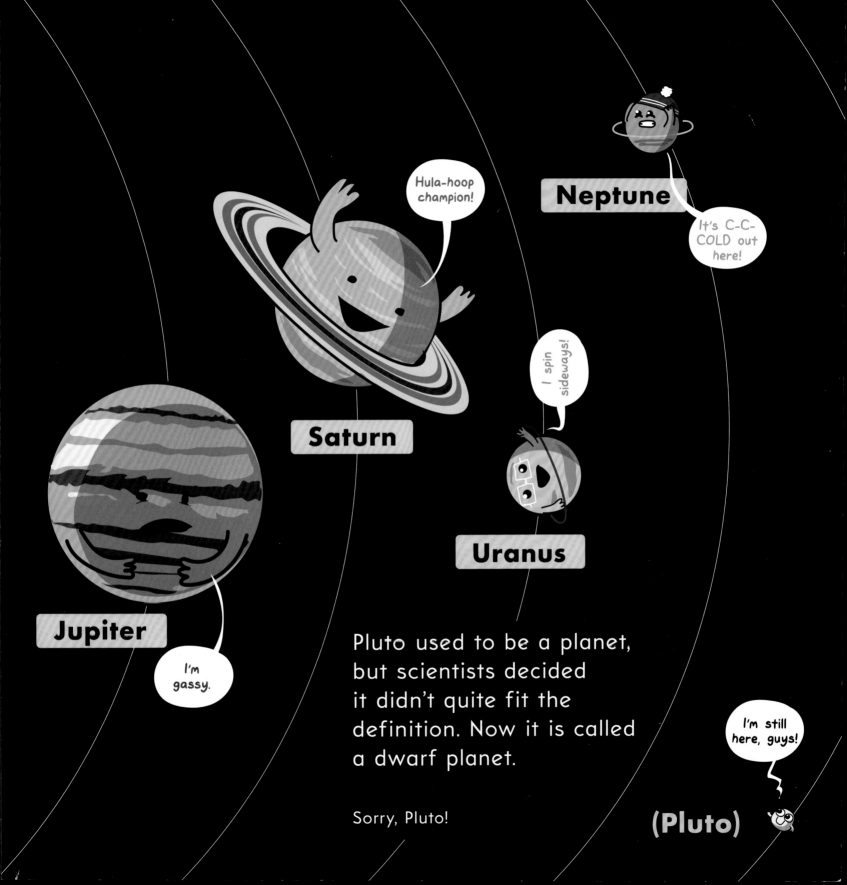

Pluto used to be a planet, but scientists decided it didn't quite fit the definition. Now it is called a dwarf planet.

Sorry, Pluto!

The planets move around the Sun like a big running track in space.

Each planet has its own special path that it follows. That's called its **orbit**.

Some planets are faster than others, but each one stays in its lane.

Do you know how many times you have been around the Sun?

Hint: how old are you?

SO WHAT DOES THE MOON DO ALL YEAR LONG?

While Earth is going around the Sun, the **moon** is spinning around Earth! The moon goes around Earth twelve or thirteen times in one year. That's about once a month. Depending on where the moon is in its **cycle**, we might only see part of it. The rest of the moon is in shadow. When we see the whole thing, it's called a full moon.

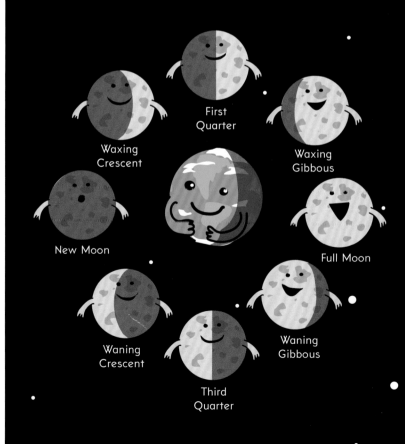

Waxing Crescent

First Quarter

Waxing Gibbous

New Moon

Full Moon

Waning Crescent

Third Quarter

Waning Gibbous

The Sun never stops
working. It does loads
of important jobs for
Earth. In fact, we wouldn't
be around without the Sun!

The Sun gives us light, so we can see, but it takes about eight minutes for light to get to us because the Sun is so far away.

It's worth the wait!

Earth spins around in a full circle every day.

NIGHT

DAY

Hi again! How was your night?

That is why when it's night-time for you, it's daytime on the other side of the world.

 OH HEY, GUESS WHAT?

As one side of Earth spins away from the Sun, it looks like the Sun is setting there, and it becomes night. As that side of Earth spins back towards the Sun, it looks like the Sun is rising, and — you guessed it — breakfast time!

The Sun is always there,
even when you can't see it.

Sometimes it looks dark outside
during the day because the Sun
is behind the clouds.

But it is still there.

Hey! Move it, clouds! I was making shadow puppets!

Once in a while, it gets dark in the daytime because the moon gets in the Sun's way.

That's called a **solar eclipse**, and it only lasts for a little while.

Keeping us warm is another really important part of the Sun's job.

The Sun is hotter than you can imagine. Way hotter than fire! Its temperature reaches MILLIONS of degrees at the centre.

Some places on Earth are warmer than others. The parts of Earth closest to the **equator** are the warmest. The parts of Earth closest to the **North** and **South Poles** are the coldest.

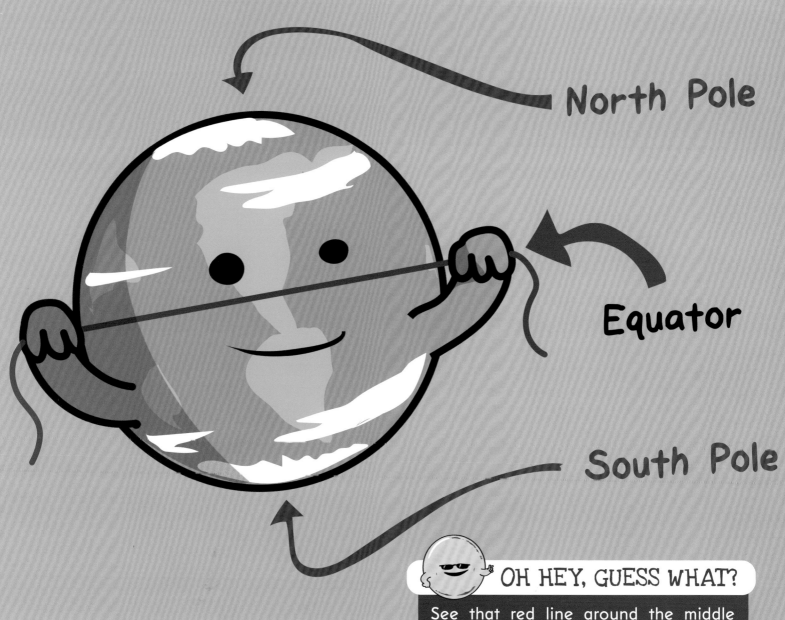

North Pole

Equator

South Pole

OH HEY, GUESS WHAT?

See that red line around the middle of Earth? It's an imaginary line people invented called the equator. It separates the top and bottom halves of Earth.

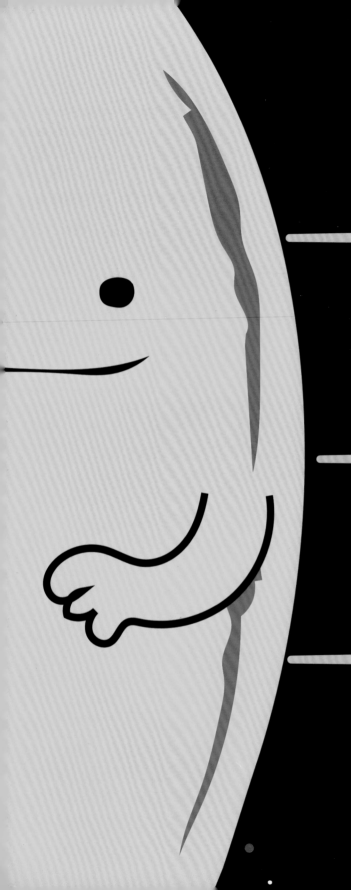

So now we know it's colder near the poles of Earth and warmer near the equator. But why?

Well, the parts of Earth near the equator are getting the Sun's heat from straight on.

The North and South Poles are getting the same amount of sunlight, but it gets spread out over a bigger area.

Since these places have to share the Sun's heat, they don't get quite as warm.

(less direct Sun)

Equator ↗
(more direct Sun)

South Pole
(less direct Sun)

While Earth is moving around the Sun, it is spinning on a tilt.

That's why we have **seasons**.

There are four seasons – spring, summer, autumn and winter.

Because of Earth's tilt, the top half and the bottom half of the world experience the seasons at different times.

When the bottom half of Earth is tilted towards the Sun, it is summer there. This also means that the top half of Earth is tilted away from the Sun, which makes it winter there.

The Sun's work isn't done yet!

Every day, the Sun also has an important job in the water cycle.

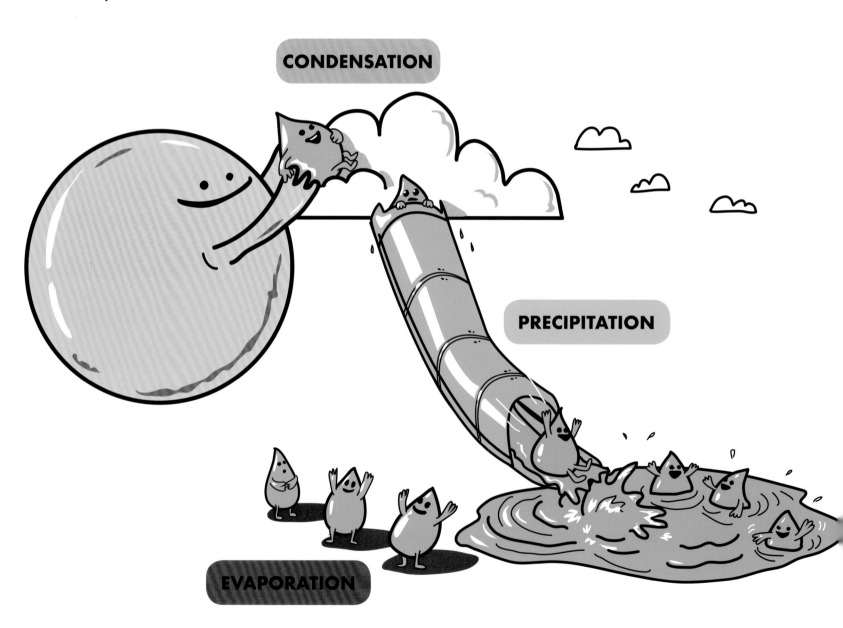

WHAT HAPPENS DURING THE WATER CYCLE?

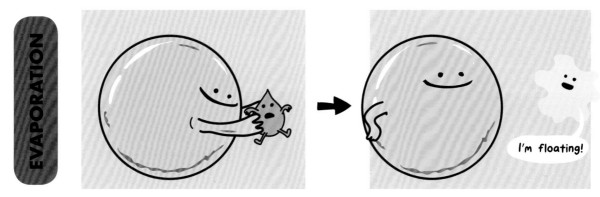

Heat from the Sun causes water to mix with air, turning into vapour. That's called **evaporation**!

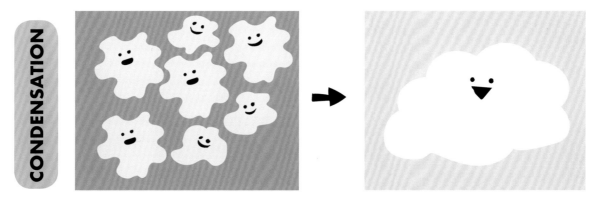

Then the vapour gathers together to make clouds. That's called **condensation**!

Finally, the water comes back down as rain or snow. That's called **precipitation**.

The water cycle is important for all living things, but especially for plants. Plants need water and sunlight for **photosynthesis**! That's a big word, but it's also a really big job.

Photosynthesis is when a plant uses light from the Sun, water from the water cycle and carbon dioxide from the air to make food for energy to help it grow.

During photosynthesis, plants make oxygen. That's what animals and people need to breathe. Take a deep breath. You just breathed in a lot of oxygen.

Oxygen doesn't have any taste, but it's always there. We can't live without it. If the Sun wasn't helping out with photosynthesis, we wouldn't have oxygen!

The Sun is pretty great.

It's always around, keeping the whole solar system together. It gives us light and keeps us warm. It helps bring us rain and grow plants to produce the oxygen we breathe.

It's such a big part of our lives that we wouldn't be able to live without it!

The Sun works *really* hard to help us out.

That's kind of a big deal.

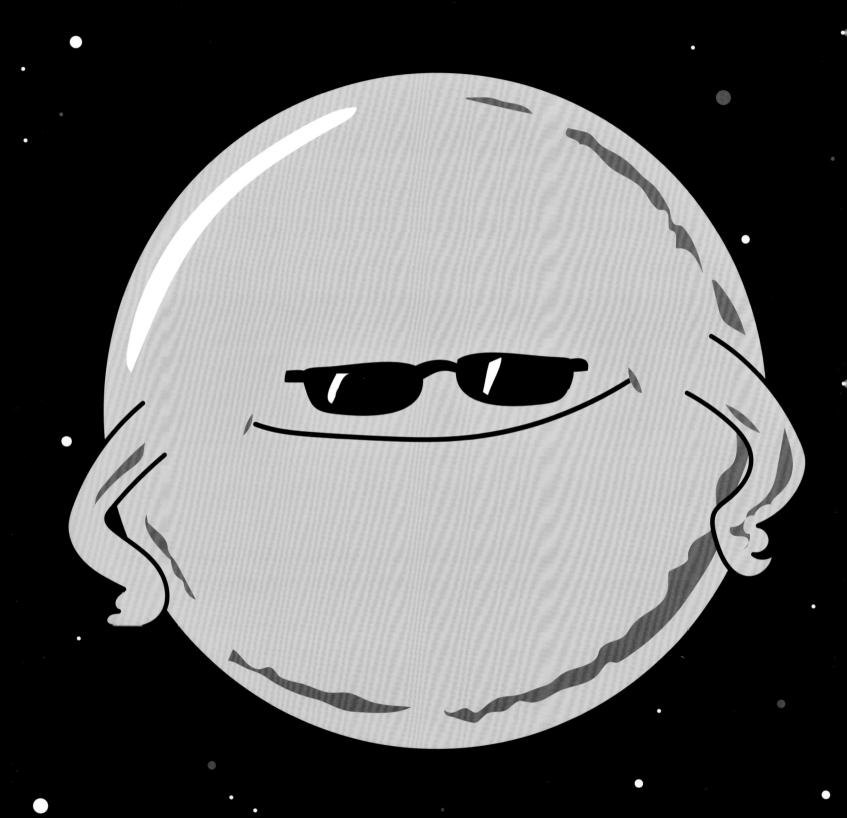

GLOSSARY

ASTEROID: A SMALL ROCKY OBJECT THAT TRAVELS AROUND THE SUN

COMET: AN ICY ROCK THAT SHOOTS THROUGH SPACE AND LEAVES A TRAIL OF GAS AND DUST

CONDENSATION: THE CHANGING OF A GAS OR VAPOUR INTO ITS LIQUID FORM

CYCLE: A SERIES OF EVENTS THAT ARE REPEATED IN THE SAME ORDER

DWARF PLANET: A ROCKY BODY IN SPACE THAT IS SMALLER THAN A PLANET BUT BIGGER THAN MOST ASTEROIDS

EQUATOR: AN IMAGINARY LINE AROUND THE MIDDLE OF THE EARTH THAT IS AN EQUAL DISTANCE FROM THE NORTH AND SOUTH POLES

EVAPORATION: THE PROCESS OF CHANGING A LIQUID INTO A VAPOUR OR GAS

GALAXY: A VERY LARGE GROUP OF STARS AND PLANETS

METEOR: A STREAK OF LIGHT CREATED WHEN A PIECE OF SPACE ROCK OR METAL SPEEDS INTO EARTH'S ATMOSPHERE

MOON: THE NATURAL SATELLITE THAT MOVES AROUND EARTH ABOUT ONCE EACH MONTH AND IS VISIBLE BECAUSE IT REFLECTS LIGHT FROM THE SUN

NORTH POLE: THE MOST NORTHERN PART OF EARTH, LOCATED AT THE TOP OF EARTH'S AXIS

ORBIT: THE CURVED PATH FOLLOWED BY A MOON, PLANET OR SATELLITE AS IT CIRCLES A PLANET OR THE SUN

PHOTOSYNTHESIS: A CHEMICAL PROCESS BY WHICH GREEN PLANTS AND SOME OTHER ORGANISMS USE ENERGY FROM THE SUN TO TURN WATER AND CARBON DIOXIDE INTO FOOD. THEY PRODUCE OXYGEN AS A BY-PRODUCT

PLANET: A LARGE, ROUND BODY IN SPACE THAT ORBITS A STAR

PRECIPITATION: THE FALLING OF WATER FROM THE SKY IN THE FORM OF RAIN, SLEET, HAIL OR SNOW

SEASON: ONE OF THE FOUR NATURAL PARTS OF THE YEAR

SOLAR ECLIPSE: A TIME WHEN THE MOON COMES BETWEEN THE SUN AND EARTH SO THAT ALL OR PART OF THE SUN'S LIGHT IS BLOCKED

SOLAR SYSTEM: THE SUN TOGETHER WITH ITS ORBITING BODIES: THE PLANETS, CIRCLED BY THEIR MOONS, AS WELL AS DWARF PLANETS, ASTEROIDS, COMETS AND METEOROIDS

SOUTH POLE: THE MOST SOUTHERN PART OF EARTH, LOCATED AT THE BOTTOM OF EARTH'S AXIS

STAR: A MASS OF BURNING GAS, SEEN IN THE SKY AT NIGHT AS A GLOWING POINT OF LIGHT

SUN: ANY STAR THAT IS THE CENTRE OF A SYSTEM OF PLANETS

DID YOU KNOW PEOPLE USED TO THINK THE SUN WENT AROUND EARTH?

In fact, a long, long time ago, people thought that the whole universe – including the Sun, moon and stars – all moved around Earth! This idea is called the geocentric model of the universe, and it's, well, wrong. An ancient astronomer named Ptolemy (TALL-o-me) is known for spreading this idea around.

It took astronomers many years of watching the way stars and planets move before realizing that the Sun is actually the *centre* of the solar system. An astronomer named Copernicus (kah-PER-nuh-cuss) is famous for making this discovery popular. It is called the heliocentric model of the universe – and it's what scientists still follow today!

DID YOU KNOW PEOPLE USED TO USE THE SUN TO TELL TIME?

Yep, that's right. For a long time, ancient people used all kinds of devices like candles and hourglasses to estimate time. Then the Egyptians started using the object we call a sundial around 1300 BC. (That's almost 3,500 years ago!) Here's how it worked: because the Sun's position changes throughout the day, the pointer would cast a shadow on an area of the face, or dial, depending on where the Sun was in the sky. This shadow told you what time it was. The sundial was pretty cool because it allowed people to break the day into different sections (kind of like we do with hours). But sundials weren't nearly as good as clocks. For instance, a sundial was useless at night because, well, there was no sunlight. Nowadays, we use clocks and phones to tell the time. But people can still estimate the time of day by looking at where the Sun is in the sky. (For example, if the Sun looks like it is almost right above you, it's around midday!) It's especially helpful if you're spending time in nature without a watch.

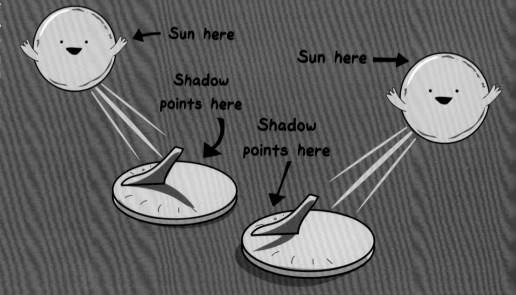

Sun here

Shadow points here

Sun here

Shadow points here

DID YOU KNOW SOME CIVILIZATIONS USED TO WORSHIP THE SUN?

Some ancient civilizations believed the Sun was a really big deal before they even fully understood it! Some Egyptian, Indo-European and Meso-American people believed the Sun was their ruler, giving them light, wisdom and justice. People didn't know the scientific explanations for why certain things happened, but they knew the Sun was a big part of it. They came up with all kinds of interesting stories about how things worked back then. For example, the ancient Greeks believed that the god Helios would pull the Sun across the sky in a chariot every morning!

DID YOU KNOW PEOPLE USED THE SUN TO PROVE THAT EARTH IS ROUND?

A very long time ago – before we had cars and aeroplanes and skateboards – it was really hard for people to travel long distances. Since everyone was stuck pretty close to home, they didn't have a lot of information about Earth. Maybe it's because Earth kind of looks flat from the ground or because when you look far off into the horizon the land seems to drop off, but people all over the world believed Earth was flat. It wasn't until about 2,500 years ago that a mathematician named Pythagoras (puh-THAH-guh-russ) argued that Earth and the moon were actually *round.* Not too much later, Aristotle, a philosopher, gave everyone real evidence to back up Pythagoras's theory. Aristotle noticed that a ship's hull disappeared first when it sailed over the horizon and that Earth cast a round shadow (not a flattened one) on the moon during a lunar eclipse. Over the years, the evidence kept piling up, and we were able to determine that Earth – along with all the other planets and stars – is in fact round.

PLANETS: THEY'RE JUST LIKE US!

We got the inside scoop from the Sun – the up-and-coming star of *The Milky Way*

First of all, congratulations – you've been on fire lately!
Not on fire, exactly *[laughs]*. But I do run pretty hot. I'm about 27 million degrees Fahrenheit (15 million degrees Celsius) at my core.

Your rise to fame has been a long time coming. How long have you been in the business?
More than 4.5 billion years!

It's a normal day – where do you find yourself?
At the centre of the solar system, surrounded by my eight planets and five dwarf planets.

Tell us something your fans might not know about you.
I'm technically a yellow dwarf star, but that doesn't mean I'm small! I'm about 2.7 million miles around (or almost 4.4 million km).

Thanks for chatting with us. It's nice to meet a star that's so down to earth.
Anything for the fans.

Could Earth be in the market for a new moon?

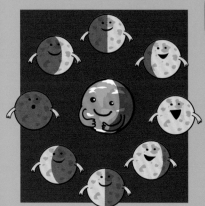

Could Earth be adding a second moon to its orbit? Earth only has one moon, but a friend says, "Earth and Mars are so competitive! Earth would love to get a second or third moon to top Mars's two!" But sources at NASA say that the change is a lot of hot air. Earth will have to stick with just the one.

IT'S BEEN A LONG DAY!

Venus kicks back after the longest day in the solar system – clocking in around 5,832 hours!

CAST REUNION!

The cast of *The Milky Way* got together to snap this sweet selfie. The solar system that spins together stays together!

SPOTTED!

Mercury, the smallest of the solar system's eight planets, was seen spinning around the galaxy with Jupiter, the largest planet, who's around 35x bigger! What a mismatched pair! But maybe with three planets between them the difference doesn't seem so big?

WHO WORE IT BETTER? RING EDITION

SATURN
72%

URANUS
25%

NEPTUNE
3%

NEW YEAR!

HAPPY NEW YEAR!

Neptune finally finished one orbit around the Sun after spinning for 60,182 Earth days! That's a wrap!

MARS SEES RED!

What has the fourth planet so angry? Sources say Mars's feud with its neighbour Earth could be heating up! "Mars wants to be left alone. But Earth's rovers keep dropping by uninvited." Rude.